11/13

THE CASE OF
The Rusty Nail

Michelle Faulk, PhD

Enslow Publishers, Inc.
40 Industrial Road
Box 398
Berkeley Heights, NJ 07922
USA

http://www.enslow.com

Library of Congress Cataloging-in-Publication Data

Faulk, Michelle.
    The case of the rusty nail : Annie Biotica solves nervous system disease crimes /
    Michelle Faulk.
        p. cm. — (Body system disease investigations)
    Includes index.
    Summary: "Learn about diseases and their symptoms such as tetanus,
West Nile virus, and botulism among others"—Provided by publisher.
    ISBN 978-0-7660-3949-0
    1. Nervous system—Infections—Juvenile literature. I. Title.
    RC359.5.F35 2013
    616.9'3—dc23   2011029275

Future editions:
Paperback ISBN 978-1-4644-0227-2
ePUB ISBN 978-1-4645-1140-0
PDF ISBN 978-1-4646-1140-7

Printed in China
062012 Leo Paper Group, Heshan City, Guangdong, China

10 9 8 7 6 5 4 3 2 1

Photo Credits: CDC: Cynthia Goldsmith, p. 16 (right), James Gathany, p. 13, Pete Seidel,
p. 35; Illustrations by Jeff Weigel (www.jeffweigel.com), pp. 1, 3, 5, 9, 13, 15, 19, 21, 25, 27,
31, 33, 37, 38, 40, 42, 47; Photo Researchers, Inc.: 3D4Medical, p. 11, A. Dowsett, pp. 22, 24
(bottom), 34 (bottom right), 37, Bjorn Svensson, p. 38, Brian Evans, p. 33, BSIP, p. 32, CNRI,
pp. 10, 28 (top), 30, 36, David M. Phillips, p. 34 (bottom left), Dr. George Lombard, p. 23, Dr.
Linda M. Stannard, University of Cape Town, pp. 16 (left), 18 (bottom), Medical Body Scans,
p. 34 (top left), Roger Harris, p. 34 (bottom middle); Shutterstock.com, pp. 6, 7, 8, 9, 12, 14,
15, 16 (top), 17, 18 (top), 19, 20, 21, 24 (top), 26, 28 (bottom), 29, 34 (top right), 41, 43.

Cover Illustration: Illustrations by Jeff Weigel (www.jeffweigel.com)

Contents

My name is **Agent Annie Biotica**. I am a Disease Scene Investigator with the Major Health Crimes Unit. My job is to keep people safe from the troublemaker germs out there. How do I do it? I use logic and the scientific method. I gather clues from health crime scenes. I identify microbe suspects. I gather evidence. If all goes well I get justice for the victims by curing them. Sometimes all doesn't go well. These are some of my stories.

Annie Biotica

The Human Nervous System

The nervous system allows the brain to communicate with the rest of the body. Messages are sent through nerves. When your hand comes close to a hot stove, nerve cells in the skin send an alarm to the brain. The brain responds by sending a message that contracts the muscles in the hand and arm. This jerks your hand away from the hot stove. The nervous system is lightning fast. By the time you are aware of the hot stove your hand has already moved.

There are two parts to the human nervous system. The central nervous system (CNS) is made up of the brain and spinal cord. The peripheral nervous system (PNS) includes all the nerves that branch off the spinal cord. The CNS is surrounded by three layers of membranes called the meninges. Cerebrospinal fluid (CSF) fills the space in between the inside and middle layer of meninges. The CSF cushions the CNS inside the skull and back bones.

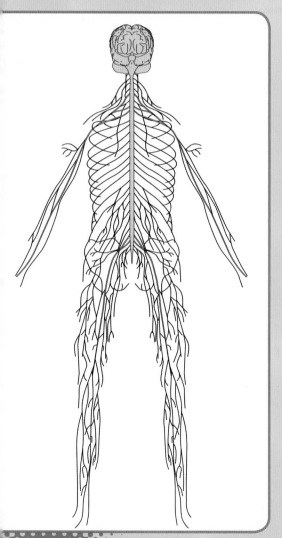

The central nervous system contains the brain and spinal cord (yellow). The peripheral nervous system contains all the nerves that branch off the spinal cord (black).

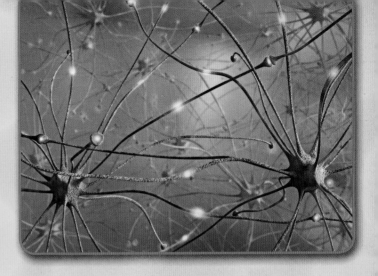

Nerves are the roadways that the nervous system uses to send messages throughout the body.

The blood-brain barrier is an area of tiny blood vessels that surround the brain. It guards and prevents things from entering the brain. Even the body's own immune system has trouble getting past this barrier. It is rare, but sometimes microbes get past this barrier. Away from the immune system they quickly multiply and cause serious diseases. When the meninges are attacked, the disease is called meningitis. If the brain is attacked the disease is called encephalitis.

When the blood-brain barrier and meninges become torn it creates a doorway for microbes. A fractured skull or brain surgery, for example, can allow this to happen.

The meninges protect the brain from invaders. During meningitis, the three layers get infected and swollen.

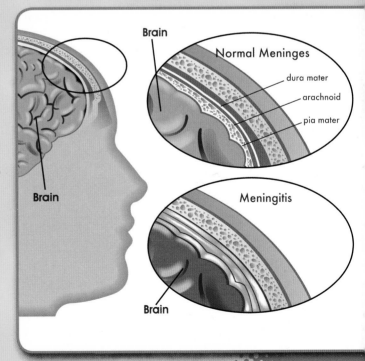

Brain

Brain

Normal Meninges
- dura mater
- arachnoid
- pia mater

Meningitis

Brain

Chapter 1

THE CASE OF
the *Rusty Nail*

The Crime

Tinisha and her two brothers Will and Marcus were visiting their grandparents' farm one summer day. Even though they had been told to stay away from the old barn, they couldn't resist. Once inside, Tinisha regretted going along. The place was filthy and smelled of animal manure. There were piles of old wood with rusty nails everywhere. Tinisha had on thin flip flops and really wanted to leave. As she crawled up an old wooden ladder to the hayloft, a huge spider web became stuck to her bare leg. Grossed out, she jumped to the barn floor. When she landed she felt a sharp pain in her heel. A week later Tinisha was in the emergency room, flip flops and all.

The Clues

When I met Tinisha in the ER these were her symptoms:

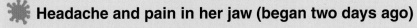

- Headache and pain in her jaw (began two days ago)
- Jaw and face muscles so stiff that she seemed to be sneering
- Stiff neck and arm muscles
- Trouble swallowing
- High blood pressure

These clues indicated a nervous system attack. When asked about recent injuries she told me about the barn escapade. I checked and saw a red spot on her heel. I also saw a small tear in her flip-flop.

The Suspects

My primary suspect was the bacterium *Clostridium tetani*. Because of the hole in Tinisha's flip-flop, I suspected a nail had punctured her heel. A deep puncture wound is a favorite doorway for *C. tetani*, a notorious bacterial offender. *C. tetani* hates oxygen and hides inside hard seed-like pods called spores. These spores are common in dirt and manure. A nail would have pushed *C. tetani* spores

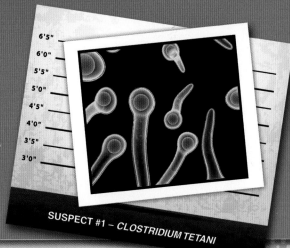

SUSPECT #1 – CLOSTRIDIUM TETANI

deep into Tinisha's skin where they would have hatched.

C. tetani produces a poison called a toxin. The tetanus toxin enters the bloodstream. It attaches to nerve cells that control muscles. The muscles cannot relax. As more muscles become tight, the victim experiences horrible pain. Some victims' muscles contract so strongly that their head bends back toward their feet! Eventually the chest muscles contract so hard that breathing becomes impossible.

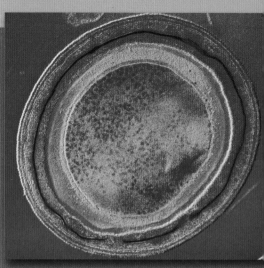

This spore was made by Clostridium tetani.

The Evidence

The clue that really caught my attention was Tinisha's sneering facial expression. This is a well-known calling card of C. tetani. There are no specific laboratory tests for tetanus. I could charge this suspect based on Tinisha's symptoms. However, I had a little trick up my sleeve.

Test One — The Gag Test

I got a long piece of licorice from the vending machine in the hospital. I had Tinisha say *Ahh* and I gently pressed on the back of her throat with the licorice. A healthy person's reaction will be to cough and gag. The jaw of a person with tetanus will bite down hard.

Result: As soon as I touched the back of Tinisha's throat her jaw snapped shut.

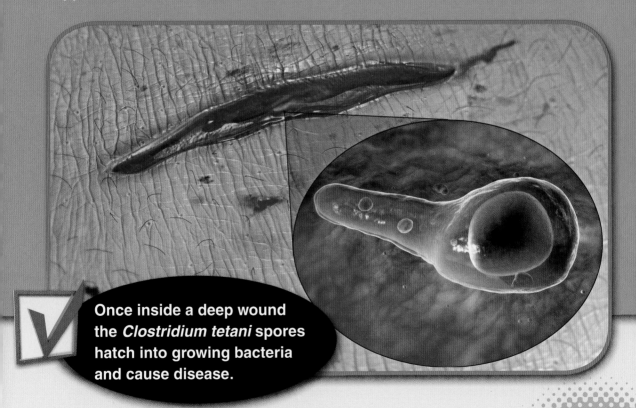

Once inside a deep wound the *Clostridium tetani* spores hatch into growing bacteria and cause disease.

The bacterium *Clostridium tetani* was found guilty on all counts of attacking Tinisha's nervous system.

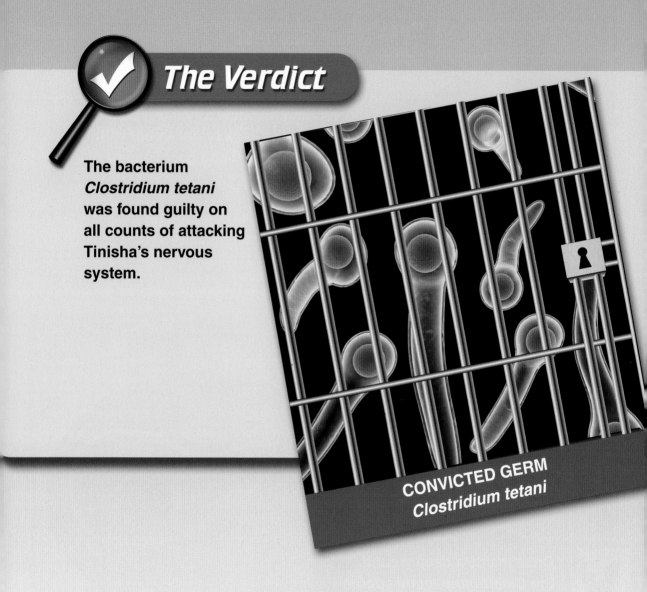

CONVICTED GERM
Clostridium tetani

Justice

Once the tetanus toxin attaches to nerve cells it cannot be removed. The toxins lose power after a week. In the meantime:

1. Tinisha was given antibiotics to kill any remaining *C. tetani* in her body.

2. She was given tetanus immune globulin (TIG). These antibodies will help prevent tetanus toxin in her body from binding to nerve cells.

3. Tinisha was given a tetanus shot because her last one was twelve years ago. People should get one every ten years. The vaccine contains tetanus toxin that has been made harmless. This would encourage her body's immune system to make even more antibodies. The vaccine also protects a person from diphtheria and whooping cough.

In time, Tinisha recovered from her attack.

A tetanus shot is a vaccine. It contains tetanus toxin that has been made harmless.

This is Agent Annie Biotica signing off. Stay safe out there.

Chapter 2

THE CASE OF
the *Deadly Mosquito Bite*

The Crime

Phalguni Gupta was very healthy at sixty-seven years old. He did not smoke or drink, and he loved the outdoors. One summer Phalguni became mysteriously ill. A few key clues helped me identify the culprit and save Phalguni.

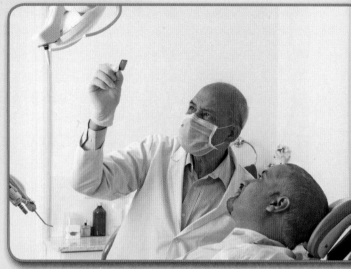

In July, Phalguni returned from a fishing trip. Two days later he woke up with intense pain in his left jaw and ear. His doctor sent him to a dentist. The dentist couldn't find any reason for the pain. During the next seven days Phalguni's condition got a lot worse. He ended up in the emergency room. These were his symptoms:

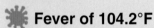 Fever of 104.2°F

Horrible pain in left side of his face

Trouble swallowing

A bad headache

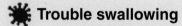 Pain behind his eyes

Phalguni was admitted to the hospital. The next day he started vomiting. He had severe weakness in all his muscles and had trouble walking. Most disturbing was that he was confused and couldn't remember things. He didn't even recognize his wife or his son.

Mosquitoes can spread viruses in their saliva.

Phalguni's symptoms came on very fast. Viruses are the microbes known for fast attacks. Because Phalguni's muscles, eyes, and mind had been affected, it was clear that his nervous system had been invaded. I was on the hunt for a virus that attacks the nervous system.

I asked Phalguni's wife what he had done right before his symptoms appeared. She said he had gone fishing. She also complained that he never used insect repellant. He had come home covered with mosquito bites.

Mosquitoes act as virus buses. They bite a wild animal that is infected with a virus. The virus rides along with the mosquito. The mosquito then passes the virus on in its saliva.

I called the State Health Department. They told me that in the area Phalguni had been fishing a large number of wild birds had been dying. Mosquitoes tested in that area had been positive for West Nile and St. Louis Encephalitis viruses. Both viruses cause zoonotic diseases. *Zoonotic* means the disease can be passed between animals, insects, and people. Both viruses use wild birds as a hideout. These two virus trespassers are especially vicious to older people. Phalguni was sixty-seven years old and experiencing a severe disease. Death was a real possibility.

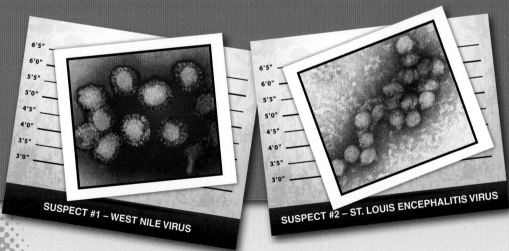

SUSPECT #1 – WEST NILE VIRUS

SUSPECT #2 – ST. LOUIS ENCEPHALITIS VIRUS

Test Blood for Antibodies

I took a sample of Phalguni's blood. I tested his blood for the presence of antibodies that recognize the West Nile or the St. Louis Encephalitis viruses.

Result: Phalguni's blood contained antibodies that recognized the West Nile virus. It did not have antibodies that recognized the St. Louis Encephalitis virus.

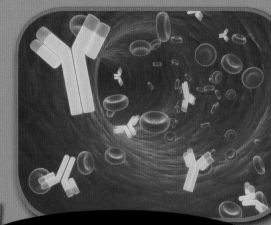

Phalguni's blood was positive for antibodies to West Nile virus.

Test CSF for West Nile Virus

The antibody test was solid evidence for West Nile virus. However, a second identification is always best. I inserted a needle into Phalguni's spine and removed

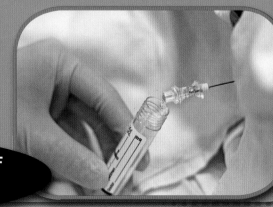

A sample of Phalguni's CSF was taken from his spine.

some of his cerebral spinal fluid (CSF). I ordered a test called a polymerase chain reaction (PCR) on the CSF. PCR uses small guided missiles called primers. The primers find the genetic material inside a virus. This test can detect very tiny amounts of virus.

Result: Phalguni's CSF contained West Nile virus.

The PCR test showed that Phalguni had the West Nile virus in his body.

 The Verdict

The West Nile virus was found guilty on all counts of causing Phalguni's disease.

CONVICTED GERM
West Nile virus

Justice

Viral attacks are very hard to stop. This is especially true when the viral offender is inside the central nervous system. All that could be done for Phalguni was to support his body while it fought off the invader. Phalguni was given food and fluids. I also called in back-up. A physical therapist came every day to help Phalguni's muscles stay strong. When Phalguni began to have trouble breathing he was put on a ventilator. Eventually Phalguni's body began to recover. It took a month but Phalguni went home. Unfortunately, his central nervous system was permanently damaged. He had to walk with a cane the rest of his life.

Phalguni lived but this viral attack left permanent scars.

This is Agent Annie Biotica signing off. Stay safe out there.

Chapter 3

THE CASE OF
the *Floppy Baby*

The Crime

A young couple took their four-month-old baby Ludvig out to their garden. Ludvig's dad let him suck on a freshly picked green bean. That night Ludvig was fussy and wouldn't take his bottle. His mom put some honey on the tip of the bottle. Ludvig liked that. It was a wonderful day for this young family. Three weeks later they were living a nightmare.

Baby Ludvig tasted a green bean from the garden.

I got the call when baby Ludvig was sent to the hospital. These were Ludvig's symptoms:

- Four days earlier he stopped going to the bathroom.

- Over the past four days he had become less active.

- He could no longer hold his head up.

- He had trouble sucking his bottle. Even his cry was weak.

- I examined Ludvig. One at a time I picked up each of Ludvig's arms and legs and let go. They flopped back onto the table.

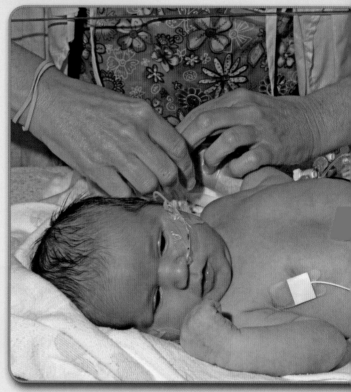

Ludvig went to the hospital.

Losing all muscle movement is called flaccid paralysis. It is the opposite of a tetanus attack, in which the muscles cannot relax. The bacterial gangster called *Clostridium botulinum* causes flaccid paralysis in babies. The paralysis is caused by a toxin released by *C. botulinum*. Babies are easily attacked by *C. botulinum* spores. Their stomachs have very little acid. They lack good protective bacteria in their gut. Their immune systems are still very weak.

I talked to the parents. I heard about Ludvig's sucking on food right from the garden. *C. botulinum* hates air and spends a lot of time inside spores. These spores are everywhere in soil. I also heard about the honey on his bottle. Babies less than one year old should not eat honey because of the possible presence of *C. botulinum* spores.

The bacterial suspect Clostridium botulinum. The pink circles are spores.

SUSPECT #1 – CLOSTRIDIUM BOTULINUM

The Evidence

Test One — Test the Feces for *C. botulinum*

I got a fecal sample from Ludvig. I smeared it on a microscope slide and performed a Gram stain. The Gram stain divides bacteria into two groups. Pink is gram negative and purple is gram positive. In any feces there will be bacteria. But will I see gram positive (purple) bacteria with spores?

Result: I saw many bacteria. However, there were a large number of gram positive bacteria in the shape of tennis rackets. These were bacteria that were creating new spores. This is exactly how *C. botulinum* looks. To be sure, I did a second test.

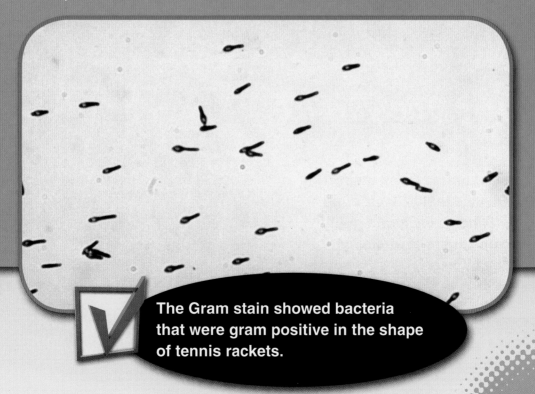

The Gram stain showed bacteria that were gram positive in the shape of tennis rackets.

Test Two — Test the Blood for Botulism Toxin

I took a blood sample from baby Ludvig. I had to use mice in this test. While I love all animals, a baby's life was at stake. I injected four mice with Ludvig's blood.

Result: The next day all four mice were dead. I tested the mice and found *C. botulinum* in all four.

The mouse test showed that Ludvig had the botulism toxin in his body.

The Verdict

Based on the Gram stain and mice tests *Clostridium botulinum* was found guilty on all counts of attacking baby Ludvig.

CONVICTED GERM
Clostridium botulinum

Justice

The problem with bacterial toxins is that once they are stuck to a nerve there is no getting them off. To help save Ludvig's life I did the following:

- I gave him antitoxin. This is botulism toxin that has been made harmless. This would help stimulate his immune system to make antibodies against the toxin. These antibodies would protect the nerve cells that had not already been attacked.

- I made sure Ludvig remained in the intensive care unit until the effects of the botulism toxin wore off.

In time Ludvig recovered and went home.

This is Agent Annie Biotica signing off. Stay safe out there.

Chapter 4

THE CASE OF
the *Crazy Raccoon*

The Crime

On a summer day, fifty-six-year-old Jacob came out of his barn to find his granddaughter petting a wild raccoon! Raccoons are night animals and not friendly with people. Something was very wrong. Jacob quietly asked his granddaughter to go in the house. She did not want to leave her new friend. As Jacob reached down to pick up the little girl the raccoon jumped up and bit his left hand.

A wild raccoon bit Jacob.

Jacob took his granddaughter inside and got his rifle. Jacob knew he had to capture the raccoon so that he could get it tested, but it was running away. He had no choice. He went outside and fired his gun.

Jacob took the raccoon to a vet. They sent it to the state's health lab to be tested for rabies. Unfortunately, the raccoon got lost in the mail. Jacob was told he should get treated for the rabies virus just to be safe. He refused. Thirty-eight days later I got the call.

The Clues

At the hospital I documented Jacob's disease:

* Five days earlier: sore throat
* Four days earlier: trouble swallowing
* Two days earlier: facial muscles kept twitching and he seemed afraid
* One day earlier: he couldn't swallow; he had to spit his saliva into a cup
* One day earlier: taken to the emergency room
* Since he had been in the hospital: a fever that came and went, itchiness, vomiting, body cramps, and pain in the muscles of the left hand; also agitation and confusion

The friendly behavior of the wild raccoon was definitely suspicious. I believed that Jacob had been attacked by the rabies virus when he was bitten. This virus hides out in many wild animals. The virus is transferred to the victim through the animal's saliva. It multiplies in the tissues near the wound. Eventually it travels along the body's nerves to the central nervous system. The target of this bullet-shaped virus is the brain. Once there it causes the brain to swell, resulting in encephalitis. The pressure on the swollen brain makes the infected animal or person behave oddly. For example, a wild animal could become very friendly. Jacob's symptoms of agitation and being afraid were also typical of a person infected with rabies.

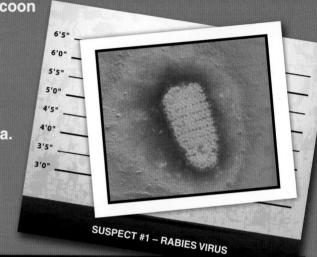

SUSPECT #1 – RABIES VIRUS

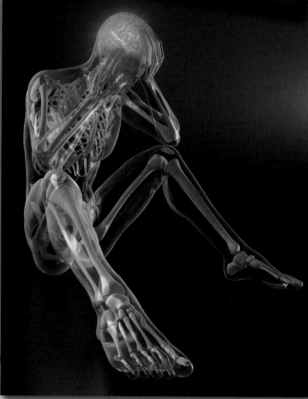

Rabies causes the brain to swell. This is called encephalitis.

The Evidence

 **The Polymerase Chain Reaction (PCR)**

To positively identify the rabies virus in this crime I began by collecting some of Jacob's saliva.

I performed the PCR test on the sample. This test uses tiny pieces of genetic material called primers. The primers are mirror images of parts of the virus' genetic material. If the rabies virus is in the sample the primers will stick to it.

Result: Jacob's saliva had the rabies virus in it.

 The PCR test proved that Jacob had the rabies virus in his body.

The Verdict

The rabies virus was found guilty on all counts of causing Jacob's disease.

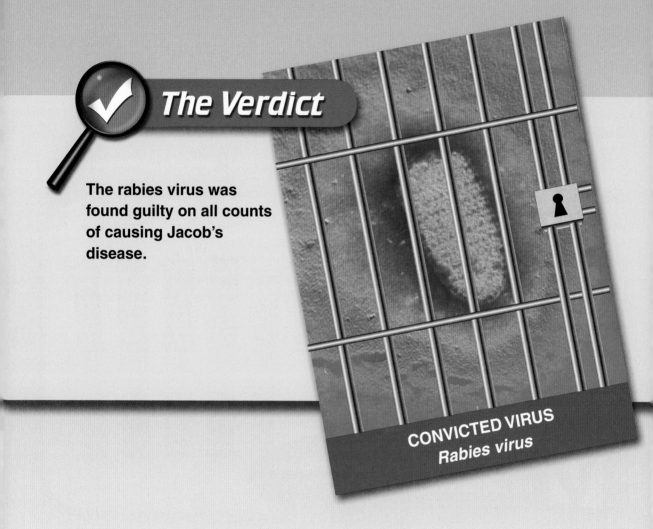

CONVICTED VIRUS
Rabies virus

Justice

It is recommended that people get treatment for rabies when they are bitten by an animal that tests positive for this viral wrongdoer. If a person is bitten by a suspicious animal that cannot be tested, he should also get treated. I really wished Jacob had agreed to be treated when the raccoon first bit him. The risk of death from rabies is much higher the longer the victim goes without treatment.

I gave Jacob the actual rabies vaccine to help his immune system target the rabies virus. After that, we could only wait and see if Jacob's immune system could fight this attack. Unfortunately, Jacob died seventeen days after his symptoms began.

This is Agent Annie Biotica signing off. Stay safe out there.

Chapter 5

THE CASE OF
the Deadly Ear Infection

The Crime

Carlos was a healthy thirteen-year-old boy when he was the victim of a misdemeanor health attack. He caught a respiratory virus that kept him in bed for a week. During this attack a complication developed. He got an earache.

The human ear has three sections: the inner, middle, and outer ear. The middle of Carlos's left ear filled with fluid. This is called otitis media.

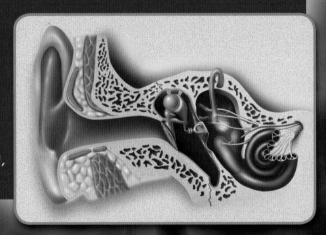

The ear has three sections: the outer (tan), the middle (purple), and the inner ear (blue).

It hurt, but the doctor did not see any evidence of a microbe growing in this fluid. Because his ear was not infected, no antibiotics were prescribed. The doctor told Carlos's mother to take him to the emergency room if he developed a headache, stiff neck, or acted strange. Six days later Carlos's eyes were vibrating in his head! That's when I got the call.

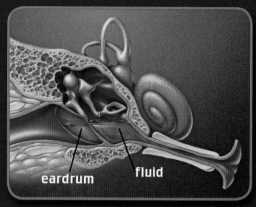

eardrum   fluid

Carlos's middle ear had fluid in it. The fluid pressed against the eardrum and caused pain.

The Clues

When I met Carlos, these were his symptoms:

- **High fever**
- **Terrible headache**
- **Intense pain in his neck when he tried to touch his chin to his chest; I also noticed that when he did this his knees moved up toward his body.**
- **Confusion**
- **Sleepiness**
- **Light hurt his eyes**
- **Vomiting**

Any patient with these symptoms may have meningitis. This means a microbial gangster has attacked the meninges. Meningitis can lead to death very quickly. We had to act now.

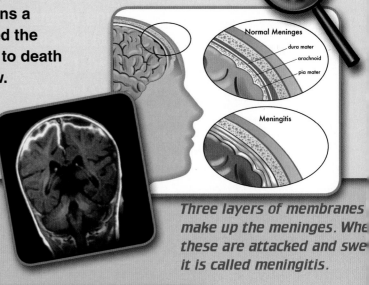

The pink lines on the right show swelling in the meninges in this patient.

Normal Meninges
dura mater
arachnoid
pia mater

Meningitis

Three layers of membranes make up the meninges. Whe these are attacked and swe it is called meningitis.

 ## The Suspects

Meningitis can be caused by bacteria, viruses, and even fungi. However, bacterial meningitis is the most deadly, so I needed to consider this possibility first. The most popular bacterial thugs that like to cause meningitis are: *Haemophilus influenzae, Streptococcus pneumoniae,* and *Neisseria meningitidis.*

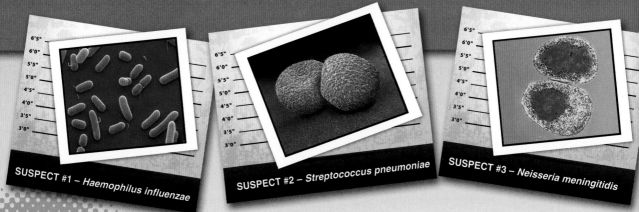

SUSPECT #1 – *Haemophilus influenzae*

SUSPECT #2 – *Streptococcus pneumoniae*

SUSPECT #3 – *Neisseria meningitidis*

The Evidence

Test One **Test CSF for Bacteria**

I took a sample of Carlos's CSF from his lower spinal cord. CSF should be clear and Carlos's was cloudy. Cloudiness can mean bacteria are present. I spread the CSF onto small dishes containing a material called chocolate agar. Agar is like gelatin. Chocolate agar contains boiled sheep's blood for the bacteria to eat. This makes it a chocolate brown color. I put the agar dishes in a warm place overnight.

Result: Bacteria grew from the CSF sample.

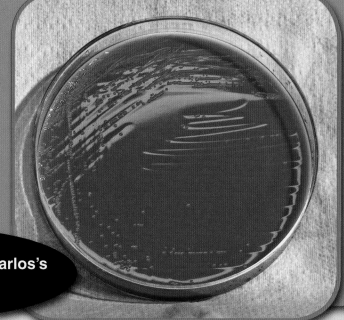

Bacteria was found in Carlos's CSF and his blood.

A Gram Stain to Identify the Bacteria

I took samples of bacteria from Carlos's CSF agar plate. I smeared the bacteria onto a glass microscope slide. I then did a Gram stain. Bacteria that stain pink are gram negative. Purple means gram positive. Staining the bacteria also allowed me to see their size and shape.

    Result: The bacteria found in Carlos's CSF were gram negative, round, and bunched together in pairs.

    I examined the mug shots of the three bacterial suspects.

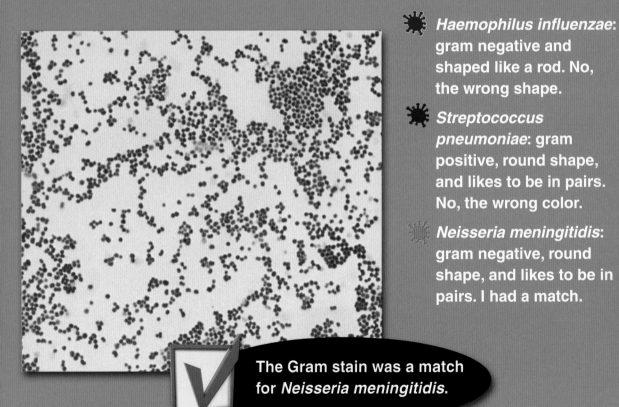

Haemophilus influenzae: gram negative and shaped like a rod. No, the wrong shape.

Streptococcus pneumoniae: gram positive, round shape, and likes to be in pairs. No, the wrong color.

Neisseria meningitidis: gram negative, round shape, and likes to be in pairs. I had a match.

The Gram stain was a match for *Neisseria meningitidis*.

The Verdict

Based on Carlos's symptoms and laboratory tests, *N. meningitidis* was found guilty on all counts of attacking Carlos's meninges.

CONVICTED GERM
Neisseria meningitidis

Justice

To treat Carlos the doctor and I agreed to use two antibiotics at once. It took several weeks but Carlos did survive his attack. Unfortunately, Carlos's disease left him deaf in both ears. One in seven people who survive bacterial meningitis are left permanently handicapped.

This is Agent Annie Biotica signing off. Stay safe out there.

You Solve the Case

A sixty-three-year-old woman was gardening on a summer day. It was so hot that she couldn't stand to have long pants on. She also couldn't find her knee pads. So she folded a towel and knelt on it. As she worked, the towel got rolled up. A lot of dirt also got onto the towel. That night when she was bathing she noticed she had many scratches and some rather deep cuts in her knees.

The Case of the Rusty Nail

Two weeks later her husband noticed her acting very strange and took her to the doctor. Her jaw hurt so bad that she was making a weird face all the time. Many of her muscles hurt and were tight. She had trouble swallowing.

- Since the woman's jaw and throat muscles are not working properly do you suspect a nervous system attack?

- As an emergency room doctor you notice the evidence of healed wounds on her knees. After talking with the husband you learn of her habit of daily gardening. What bacterial criminal is very common in dirt and can cause a serious disease?

- How does this bacteria attack the muscles?

- What treatment do you recommend?

You Solve the Case

CASE #2

A seven-year-old girl has suffered from a sinus infection for almost a month now. The doctor believed at first that it was allergies. When the girl began to sneeze out brown mucus he decided it was a bacterial infection. He prescribed antibiotics. A week later the girl was back in the office. She was having trouble balancing. She almost fell getting onto the exam table. He immediately asked if she had pain in either ear. She said her right ear had started bothering her a day or so ago. The doctor examined her ears and noticed that one was inflamed and contained fluid. There was no evidence of bacteria growing in the ear.

If an ear contains fluid but does not appear infected should antibiotics be given?

The doctor decided to keep the patient on the same antibiotics longer. He told the mother to go to the emergency room if the girl developed a bad headache, fever, stiff neck, or seemed confused. Three days later the doctor got a call from the local emergency room. The little girl had all four of these symptoms.

What disease do you suspect?

What types of microbial criminals cause this disease?

You Solve the Case

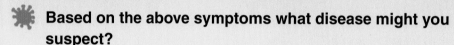

As a health investigator you've been called to the home of a six-year-old boy. He was acting very strange. His jaw hurt. He kept spitting because he had so much trouble swallowing. He seemed very nervous and afraid. He was also having fits of anger. He would kick and punch and even try to bite. His parents just didn't know what to do.

☀ Based on the above symptoms what disease might you suspect?

You ask the parents if the child had been bitten by an animal recently. They say no. Then his parents decide to mention that the little boy kept drinking out of the birdbath in the backyard. A neighbor woman often babysat him and thought it was funny. They tried to keep him away from the birdbath but he kept trying to drink from it.

☀ Do you suspect West Nile virus because the boy drank from a birdbath?

Next the parents told you that at night wild raccoons would drink from the birdbath.

☀ What disease might you suspect?

☀ What treatment is recommended?

You Solve the Case: The Answers

CASE #1 Tetanus

Since the woman's jaw and throat muscles are not working properly do you suspect a nervous system attack? Yes.

As an emergency room doctor you notice the evidence of healed wounds on her knees. After talking with the husband you learn of her habit of daily gardening. What bacterial criminal is very common in dirt and can cause a serious disease? Clostridium tetani causes the disease tetanus.

How does this bacteria attack the muscles? Bacterial cells in the body produce a toxin that prevents the muscles from relaxing.

What treatment would you give? Antibiotics, tetanus immune globulin, and tetanus vaccine.

CASE #2 Meningitis

If an ear contains fluid but does not appear infected should antibiotics be given? No. This girl was given more antibiotics because her sinus infection had not improved.

What disease do you suspect? Meningitis.

What types of microbial criminals cause this disease? Viruses, fungi, and bacteria.

CASE #3 Rabies

Based on the above symptoms what disease might you suspect? Rabies

Do you suspect West Nile virus because the boy drank from a birdbath? No. West Nile virus is transmitted through mosquito bites.

What disease might you suspect? You might again suspect rabies.

What treatment is recommended? A rabies test first. If that is positive then rabies antitoxin and the rabies vaccine could be given.

Glossary

agar: A gelatin substance high in sugar and made from red algae. It gives bacteria a place to grow and food to eat.

antibiotics: Medicines that inhibit the growth of bacteria.

antibodies: Y-shaped proteins made by the immune system to fight microbial invaders.

antitoxin: Bacterial toxin that has been made harmless. It is used to stimulate antibody production in the victim.

bacterial spores: Hard, seed-like pods that some bacteria make to survive hostile environments.

blood-brain barrier: Tiny blood vessels around the brain.

central nervous system (CNS): The brain and spinal cord.

cerebrospinal fluid (CSF): A fluid in the CNS that cushions the brain and spinal cord.

encephalitis: Swelling of the brain.

flaccid paralysis: Paralysis that occurs because the muscles cannot contract.

intensive care unit (ICU): A part of the hospital where seriously ill patients are watched very closely in case they have breathing or heart problems.

meninges: Three layers of protective cell membranes that cover the CNS.

meningitis: A disease caused by microbes attacking the meninges.

nerves: Fibers used to send signals throughout the nervous system.

Glossary

otitis media: A condition that occurs when the middle ear fills with fluid, causing an earache.

peripheral nervous system (PNS): All the nerves that branch off the spinal cord.

polymerase chain reaction (PCR): A very sensitive test that uses primers to detect microbial invaders.

primers: Small pieces of RNA or DNA that find and stick to the genetic material of a microbe.

tetanus shot: A vaccine made of tetanus toxin that has been made harmless.

toxin: A bacterial poison.

zoonotic: A microbe that can infect and cause disease in both animals and people.

Further Reading

Calamandrei, Camilla. *Fever.* Tarrytown, N.Y.: Marshall Cavendish Benchmark, 2009.

Klosterman, Lorrie. *Meningitis.* New York: Benchmark Books, 2006.

Piddok, Charles. *Outbreak: Science Seeks Safeguards For Global Health.* Washington, DC: National Geographic, 2008.

Sfakianos, Jeffrey N. *West Nile Virus.* New York: Chelsea House, 2005.

Snedden, Robert. *Fighting Infectious Diseases.* Chicago: Heinemann Library, 2007.

Internet Addresses

Centers for Disease Control and Prevention (CDC). "West Nile Virus." <http://www.cdc.gov/ncidod/dvbid/westnile/index.htm>

National Association of School Nurses. "Voices of Meningitis." <http://www.voicesofmeningitis.org/>

Index

A
agar, 35
antibiotics, 13, 33, 37 40, 44
antibodies, 13, 17, 25
antitoxin, 25, 44

B
blood-brain barrier, 7
botulism, 24, 25
brain, 6, 7, 28

C
central nervous system (CNS), 6, 18
cerebrospinal fluid (CSF), 6, 17, 35, 36
Clostridium botulinum (*C. botulinum*), 22, 23, 24
Clostridium tetani (*C. tetani*), 9-10, 12, 13, 44

E
ear, 32
encephalitis, 7, 16, 17, 28, 29

F
flaccid paralysis, 22

G
Gram stain, 23, 24, 36

H
Hemophilus influenzae, 34, 36

M
meninges, 7, 37
meningitis, 7, 34, 37, 44
mosquito, 14, 16, 44

N
Neisseria meningitidis, 34, 36, 37
nerves, 6, 10, 25, 28
nervous system, 6, 9, 16, 44

O
otitis media, 32

P
peripheral nervous system (PNS), 6
polymerase chain reaction (PCR), 18, 29

R
rabies, 27, 28, 30, 44

S
scientific method, 4
sinus infection, 40, 44
spores, 22, 23, 24
St. Louis Encephalitis virus, 16, 17
Streptococcus pneumoniae, 34, 36

T
tetanus, 10, 11, 13, 22, 44
toxin, 10, 13, 22, 24, 25, 44

V
vaccines, 13, 31, 44

W
West Nile Virus, 16, 17, 18, 42, 44

Z
zoonotic disease, 16